MW01245964

THE THRILLS AND CHILLS OF LEADERSHIP

LEADING BEYOND THE PAYCHECK

ANTIQUA BRADLEY-HUNTER, ED.D

ISBN: 978-8-218-31430-9

Printed in the United States of America

Published by AB Hunter Consulting USA, LLC.

Editor: L.B. Cadogan

DEDICATION

This book is dedicated to those who aspire to break glass ceilings and create pleasurable environments in leadership. I honor your commitment, strength and determination. The world will be a better place because of your integrity and headship. Onward and upward!

ACKNOWLEDGMENTS

Thank you to:

God, my strength and co-writer

Demetric Hunter, my husband and motivator

JonRye Hunter, my SonShine on a cloudy day

Family, Friends, and Co-Laborers in Education.

TABLE OF CONTENTS

DR. HUNTER'S EXPERIENCES:

Position	Years of Experience
Teacher	6 Years
Reading Specialist	21 Years
Administrator/Principal	4 Years
Assistant College Professor	3 Years
School Turnaround Specialist/ Consultant	3 Years
State Director of Field Implementation	2 Years
State Educational Consultant	5 Years
State Coordinator (Students Experiencing Homelessness and Parent and Family Engagement Programs)	5 Years

INTRODUCTION

I f you are going to lead, lead with a purpose. If you are going to be in charge, be the head of the best. Most importantly, if you are up for the leadership challenge, make sure you have conditioned yourself to lead with excellence because your leadership alone can build unimaginable movements or kill dreams upon arrival. Never underestimate the POWER of leadership. While the title "leader" echoes solitary, impactful leadership cannot be achieved single-handedly. Leaders are not born perfect or all-knowing, however, through proper mentorship, planning, research and dedication, success will be attained. Therefore, make sure you are prepared, well-informed, in shape and ready for the task at hand. Keep first things first, which should always be the "WHY" behind what you do.

Throughout my life I have been fortunate to lead in various sectors, ranging from college sorority president to community activist to school administrator and now to leading my own consulting practice. There were times when I wanted the leadership position and times when I didn't. During the times that I didn't, the title of leader was bestowed upon me so I had to rise to the occasion. In fact, my earliest recollection of leadership started when I was tasked with mentoring and organizing youth activities across multiple churches that formed an association. This was uncharted territory for me, but it ignited and highlighted a skillset I didn't know I possessed. From that moment on, leadership captivated me, and I had no other choice but to cultivate it and grow!

I learned many lessons along the way, but the most important lesson was that before beginning any new endeavor, one must take the time to prepare themselves mentally, physically and spiritually, which most would call conditioning. Conditioning is the groundwork that must occur before anything else can happen. Taking the time to become properly conditioned allows the leader to adequately lay the foundation for interminable success and avoid killing their dreams and the dreams of others. The proper conditioning does not only allow the leader to equip the organization and employees with the tools to operate effectively, but during the process, the leader becomes GROUNDED in who they are and develops quality leadership skills that will transcend no matter where they go. In fact, leaders should be so conditioned that they have the ability to influence a person without even thinking about it, that's leadership! This book is designed to be a preparation tool that will condition aspiring leaders to lead at transformational levels while also sharing the thrills and chills of leadership. Although the target audience is principals and administrators in an educational setting, the highpoints are all-inclusive and could be applicable to any leadership position.

CHAPTER 1

TO BE OR NOT TO BE: THE CALL TO LEADERSHIP

G raduation was great! The summer round of interviews yielded you the perfect teaching job, and the last motivational poster was hung in your new electrifying classroom. Then it was time to get to work and prove to all that you could be the best teacher ever. You were so excited about becoming Sarah and Johnny's new teacher for the upcoming school year. You read every preparation book, attended several new teacher conferences, and even sent home welcome letters to the anxious parents. You truly felt you were ready to conquer the masses and teach forever. In fact, one year later, when you were asked, "Why do you teach?", your response was, "I teach because I love it! I teach because I love to see the light bulb go off when Johnny finally gets it. I teach because I enjoy making a difference." Yes, it was understood that you needed more money, more time and more support, but your needs during that time were never stronger than your love for your students, and you wouldn't dare consider another profession. Therefore, you stayed. One year, two years, three years, four years, then five, and now what? It's five years later, and you now feel you have mastered your craft and begin to contemplate your future in education. So what's next?

Conditioning Tip #1: Prepare for the shift.

Most people begin their careers full of passion and great expectations, but as time progresses and personal growth occurs, one may find themselves at a crossroad. What's next? Remember, growth becomes parallel to expansion so prepare!

The scenario above explains the thoughts of many novice educators, but it does not limit itself to just teachers. Whether you are a nurse, lawyer, business owner, preacher, cosmetologist or musician, you quickly realize what you ANTICIPATED in your new occupation or field and what you RECEIVED are two different things. However, no matter what the profession may be, there are always circumstances one may face that could possibly provoke them to leave. But because of their passion for what they do, they choose to remain in the profession and ask themselves the million-dollar question, "What's next?"

The question "What's next?" is not an unhealthy inquiry and should be welcomed by all. It is a question that sparks a person to reflect on past performances and ignites them to set future goals. The question "What's next?" diminishes the opportunity for complacency. It allows for a plan of action to be evaluated and urges continual movement one way or another.

During the "*What's next?*" phase, one may find the need to improve, stay or change course. For example, after dating someone for a period of time, one will come to the point of asking the question "What's next?" At that time, a decision must be made whether to continue in the relationship by committing or terminate the relationship after acknowledging that it isn't working. Another example would be a high school athlete in his/her senior year. As the end of the year approaches, the question "What's next?" surfaces. The senior must make a decision to continue to compete as an athlete at the collegiate level and seek recruitment or discontinue the sport. For some, the reflection/evaluation time comes faster than others, however, it is inevitable. Failing to ask the question "What's next?" is like building a house without a blueprint; there is no plan for the way ahead.

Once a teacher has made the decision to continue in the education profession, two major options present themselves: 1) to stay, accept the pros and cons of teaching, and retire at that level or 2) move into the administration field and seek a leadership position. Either decision will yield great results, but it must be compatible with the desires of that person and no one else. Simply put, different career paths are chosen because people have different aspirations. There are some people who would never want to take on an administrative role and others who were born to be a leader. Different strokes for different folks!

For those who decide to stay in the field and remain a devoted classroom teacher, those individuals are certain they don't want to do anything other than teach, and the education system is grateful for them. In fact, without the veteran teachers there would be little experience to nurture the novice ones. There is a need for those who will remain in the classroom for the long haul.

On the other hand, for those who answered the "What's next?" question with the need to advance in their careers, their answer could have been, "I definitely want to stay in the education field, but I don't want to be a 20-, 25-, or 30-year veteran classroom teacher." Therefore, these individuals choose the path of leadership. Most administrative-driven teachers believe they have more to offer than exclusively teaching students. They have mastered the art of writing effective lesson plans, taught thought-provoking lessons year after year, graded piles of papers, led the team as department head and inadvertently completed many of the tasks assigned to the principal without the official title. Yes, these individuals knew they had come to a level of mastery as a teacher and needed to continue to grow and challenge themselves as a leader. So, they studied hard to pass the certification test, interviewed well and was awarded the opportunity to serve in the capacity as a "New Principal." Cheers to the new role and to new beginnings!

Many believe moving into administration will be an easy transition because they have spent many undocumented hours preparing by reading books, taking classes, etc. However, entering administration or any leadership position resembles the same initial process as a beginning teacher. Nothing prepares you more for the journey than hands-on experience. Although this book will give you tons of valuable insight and share common experiences to look forward to, you will learn your most important lessons day by day. Every day will be filled with new experiences.

Pathway to Leadership

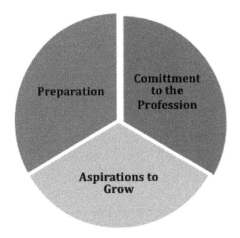

DR. HUNTER'S CORNER

My "What's next?" moment came quicker than I envisioned, arriving during my 6th year of teaching. Yes, those fun-loving 8th graders challenged me as a person, but the principal at that time ignited the fire of leadership within me due to their lack of effective leadership in education.

Discipline within the school was out of control, teachers were stressed and the staff morale was extremely low. Because of my natural desire to always search for ways to make situations better, I developed a leadership organization for girls, which improved discipline and began to explore my own leadership options. The next year, I became a principal and guess who came to the job fair looking for a job????

My takeaway from that challenging time in my career is that you can learn something from anybody, even if it's what not to do. Also, always look for ways to grow in any situation. Experiences that may make you feel uneasy can actually be the push you need to elevate to the next level.

Questions To Ask Yourself As You Reflect on Chapter 1:

Q1: Why do I want to be a leader?

Q2: In what areas of being a leader do I feel most prepared and what are my initial fears or concerns about becoming a leader?

CHAPTER 2

RESPONSIBILITIES AND ACCOUNTABILITY

D ecisions are made every day, all day in the field of education. In fact, Alyson Klien reminds readers in an Education Week article that the average classroom teacher makes at least 1,500 educational decisions a day. However, there will be no decision more important than the decision to become a leader. When one has decided to take on a leadership role, they must ensure they are pursuing the position for all the right reasons. Becoming a leader is much more than saying "I did it because it was the next thing to do," or "I have a legacy in my family," or "others told me I should do it" or "I wanted to make more money." There must be passion, commitment and a greater cause than you, when you assume the position.

A *leader* is-
a person who influences a group of people towards the achievement of a goal.

A *principal-* a person who has controlling authority or is in a leading position of a school.

You should become a leader because you want to be at the forefront of positive change that will grow the organization. You should become a leader because you believe you have the necessary skills to build up the organization and take it to the next level. You should become a leader because you can influence others and can build their capacity by empowering them to be their best. In fact, the deeper you get into leadership, you will find that it is not about you at all. Yes, the money will increase, but so will the bills and the problems. The old adage says, "To whom much is given, much is required." Your desire to become a GREAT leader must be so strong it pushes you to grow and be better today than you were yesterday. Your commitment has to be fervent enough where you will see the benefits of giving 110% of yourself when sometimes receiving nothing in return and be accepting of it. The greater good must be your staying power, which should always be the kids! In fact, there will be many times when you feel like quitting, but you must always remember the reason why you started.

So, now you have the position, the pay raise and a new office,
What's next?
How do you lead beyond the paycheck?

Although this book will identify areas you will need to condition when training to become a leader, no one can truly prepare themselves for the weight of any new leadership position, especially the principalship until you are in the position. There have been many printed How-To Manuals and Principal 101 books, but nothing gets you 100% conditioned for the level of commitment that is required of you when you take on the job of a principal. There will be many long days and short nights when taking on the role as a principal/leader.

As a teacher, you are responsible for your set of students, accountable to your set of parents and the principal of the school. However, as a principal, you become an instant glorified middleman. You are responsible for the entire student population, which may vary depending on the school's size, which could approximately range from 100-2000 students. Each of those students have parents you will be accountable to and must keep informed via newsletters, emails or phone calls. Parents must be kept abreast about the latest events or happenings at the school, discipline issues, academic decisions, programs, etc.

You are also accountable to superintendents of personnel, operational services, curriculum, etc. The range of accountability is wide and the scope of it is deep. It gets to the point where the system of just being accountable becomes a system within itself. If you're lucky, you may be able to work in a district/school system where there is less bureaucracy (fewer channels to go through). Be prepared either way!

The responsibilities of a principal are important. Overall, the main job is to supervise the total operation of the school, providing leadership and guidance and creating a professional and productive atmosphere where students can learn. More specifically, principals in collaboration with teachers establish and implement the vision, mission and goals of the school. They promote positive school culture, while providing an effective instructional program and ensure continuous professional learning is transpiring with all staff members and best practices are utilized. They also manage the organizational structure, lead personnel and manage resources. Principals collaborate with families and other community members, respond to interests and needs, and mobilize community resources. Supervisory responsibilities may include interviewing and training employees; planning, assigning and directing work; appraising performance; addressing complaints and resolving issues. No matter what position you hold, it is important to have a clear understanding of your responsibilities because knowing and doing your job will determine how others rate your effectiveness. If you are unaware of what is required in the new position and are not fulfilling the expected duties, others may view you as inadequate, not because of poor performance, but because of the lack of knowledge. So it is crucial to know your job.

In addition to the duties listed on the job description, principals take on so many added tasks and roles. Effective principals become an instant counselor to students, parents and staff, a friend, a boss, an investigator, an event planner, a protector, a cheerleader, a politician and the list goes on. No one understands the weight of the position unless they are in it, so your best confidants will not be your spouse or friends as they will not fully understand what you are going through. Your greatest resource will be other administrators who live their daily lives in the hustle and bustle just like you. Although there may be a ton of responsibilities and demands that are married with the position, there is no other profession where you meet so many people on a daily basis and have the ability to change their lives because of who you are and the access you have. The rewards are numerous, but it comes at a cost. One must not waste their opportunity to make an impact and change lives for the better during their tenure as principal/leader. Seize every moment.

Conditioning Tip #2: Know your role and be a planner.

There will be so many things to do in one day such as attending administration meetings, conducting evaluations, hosting parent conferences and handling discipline situations! Remember you are one person, and you cannot do it all in one day. Make lists to help with follow through. If you keep it in your head, you will forget. Allow others to handle minute situations. This will be your saving grace! Delegate, delegate, delegate!

Leading Beyond the Paycheck:

The Additional Roles of Effective Leaders

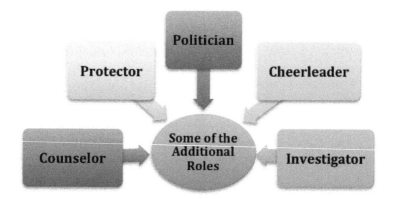

DR. HUNTER'S CORNER

In order to survive in a leadership role, you MUST learn how to delegate. Delegation was hard for me at first. I am very particular about how things should be done and lived by the saying, "If you want something done right, you have to do it yourself." But what is this statement truly communicating? When you think about it, you are diminishing the skill sets of those who support you. As a principal, I had to abandon this train of thought because at the end of my workday, I was exhausted! I knew I could not continue on this path and still show up excited and innovative each day. Plus, I had to acknowledge I didn't know it all. Once I began to build a team of high flyers, the load became lighter. I coached them and built their capacity in the areas I felt needed strengthening. Soon they began to be well-rounded thinkers, visionaries and team players who in many cases, led the school at optimal levels. As a leader you can't be afraid to share your platform. This is the sign of a great leader.

Questions To Ask Yourself As You Reflect on Chapter 2:

Q1: What duties am I most comfortable with as a leader? And What areas do I need more assistance in?

Q2: Am I efficient at multitasking? If so, how do I know? If not, what do I need to do to get better?

Q2a: What strategies will aid me in the process of multitasking?

Q3: Am I capable of delegating work to others? If so, what evidence do I have? If not, what is my plan to get started?

Q4: Do I work well under pressure? If so, how do I know? If not, what do I need to do to improve?

CHAPTER 3

KNOW YOURSELF: THE DIFFERENT TYPES OF LEADERSHIP

N ow that you know who and what you are responsible for in your new position, you will also have to be attentive to the type of leader you'll want to be. The basis for your decision should come from the core of who you are as a person. Having the ability to bring out the best in others is critical when leading a group of people. Knowing yourself, the good, the bad and the ugly is important in this process of being an effective leader. You must be able to minimize the bad and the ugly and maximize the good. No one is perfect! One of the most important traits as a leader is the ability to be consistent, and the only way to remain consistent is to be who you truly are at your core. The three most common types of leadership styles are authoritative, democratic, and laissez faire.

In short, the authoritative leader has clear expectations for what needs to be done. In fact, they know when and how it should be done. Authoritarian leaders make decisions independently with little or no input from the rest of the group and could be perceived as a dictator by others because of their self-governing mentality. Most authoritarian leaders are very detail-oriented and particular.

On the other hand, democratic leaders make followers feel important. They focus on the goals of the group as a whole and prefer joint decision-making. The democratic leader is very concerned about inclusiveness and strives for cohesiveness. Most democratic leaders are not afraid of delegation and seek new ideas from others.

Lastly, the laissez faire leader offers little to no guidance to the group. In fact, they leave most of the decision-making to the group. They trust their counterparts and believe they will make the best decisions, but their hands-off approach could be perceived as passive or unconcerned.

No matter which type of leadership style one may possess, it is important to understand that no one uses one type of leadership style all the time. John C. Maxwell, in the *5 Levels of Leadership*, explains that in many cases, leadership styles become situational, meaning different situations will dictate the type of leader that is needed at that time to be more accommodating and effective to the group. However, everyone will find themselves in one of the three categories more often than others, so there will be one leadership style that prevails over the others. Don't be afraid to identify your style.

As one goes through the year, leaders may find that at times it may be better to be laissez faire in their approach due to the minor significance of a situation or decision. It is important to pick your battles. Time is valuable and you will not be able to give your undivided attention to every problem, all the time. An example would be: What name should the grade level groups be assigned for the pep rally? That decision can be made at the lowest level possible.

There will be times when a decision will have to be made and there is no time to gather the leadership team or the faculty together to receive input. So, the leader may have to operate in an authoritarian manner and make an executive decision. However, solo decisions should be limited as much as possible. On the other hand, some teachers would prefer the leader to be able to make decisions without always calling a meeting or involving them in the process. Most teachers would rather focus on their classrooms. No matter what the situation may be, trust is a major factor when it comes to decision-making. The more the staff trusts you, the less they want to be involved with every decision. They believe that as the leader you will make the best decision for the greater good. Alternatively, there will be teachers who would rather be included in all decisions. So, as a leader you will have to find balance between the two. Overall, leadership styles will have to be adjusted based on the situation and the needs of the building, however the main goal is to establish a professional learning community where the faculty collaborates, shows unity and feels valued. As a leader it is important to know the building's needs and respond accordingly. It is also critical that in everything you do, always ask yourself what is best for the students and what is fair for everyone? There should never be hidden agendas. Todd Whitaker in his book, *17 Things that Great Teachers Do Differently*, reminds us to ask ourselves what will the best people think about your decision? If you use those three questions as your guide, and accurately self-reflect, you cannot go wrong.

Conditioning Tip #3: *Be true to who you are and be confident with your decisions.*

Most people strive to be democratic leaders most of the time. Be aware that although you may operate in a democratic manner, some will still feel that it is authoritarian because of their opinion of what democratic looks like. Opinions will vary, but do not seek the popularity vote. Do what is right and you will never go wrong.

Being Yourself

You must learn that you cannot be loved by all people.

You can be the finest apple in the world - ripe, juicy, sweet, succulent - and

offer yourself to all.

But you must remember that there will be people who do not like apples.

You must understand that if you are the world's finest apple, and someone

you love does not like apples, you have the choice of becoming a banana.

But you must be warned that if you choose to become a banana you will be a

second-rate banana.

But you can always be the finest apple.

You must also realize that if you choose to be a second-rate banana.

There will be people who do not like bananas.

Furthermore, you can spend your life trying to become the best banana

- which is impossible if you are an apple - or you can seek again to be the

finest apple.

Author Unknown

DR. HUNTER'S CORNER

If I had to give one piece of advice to novice leaders, it would be, "Don't sell your soul." You must remain true to who you are at the core. You were selected to be in the position because of qualities you possess, so why change the very thing that made you stand out in the first place? It's natural to want to be liked by all, but remember, everyone's likes are different, so how can you clearly fill everyone's desires?

As a principal in a new environment, teachers had to adjust to me the same way I had to adjust to their many personalities. My leadership style was different from the former principal, so some adjusting was needed on both sides. Most would have described me as a strict but fair leader. In fact, some teachers couldn't adjust to my level of accountability, so they left the building. Despite this, I never wavered in the overall mission, which was to improve the school, and my actions yielded me favorable and effective district evaluations, minimal discipline issues and improved test scores. Additionally, the school ended up winning the Spirit Award for the entire district!

So stay the course. Results will come. You have to be okay with not being "liked" by some and stay focused on the main thing. Be confident in who you are and stand strong, yet reflective and flexible when needed. Evaluate your leadership style regularly and always seek ways to improve to get the best results.

Questions To Ask Yourself As You Reflect on Chapter 3:

Q1: Who am I as a person?

Q2: What leadership style reflects my personality most of the time and why?

Q3: What are my non-negotiables as a leader?

Q4: Am I capable of adjusting my leadership style when necessary? How will I know when it is time to modify?

CHAPTER 4

BUILDING SOLID FOUNDATIONS: GETTING TO KNOW YOUR EMPLOYEES AND THEIR PERSPECTIVES

Before starting any new position, it is good to know who you'll be working with and the status of the organization before developing your agenda or plan for improvement. Take the time to build rapport with your employees and find out their perspective of strengths and weaknesses of the organization. You can either meet with them individually or use surveys to gather vital information. It is highly suggested that before starting your official first day on the job, you establish a way to informally introduce yourself to the staff. The staff will greatly appreciate this gesture. They are just as concerned and anxious to meet you and know your expectations as you are about being their new leader. Some creative ways would be a quick meet and greet after work, a weekend barbeque at the school or community park, or if time does not permit, feel free to send a mailed letter or email including your picture, background information, general experiences, credentials and family information (marital status, children, pets, etc.)

to connect on a personal level. Also expressing your excitement to meet them and gathering their input for the way ahead is a must. Although most administrators prefer to be hired during the summer, every start date is different. Some principals are hired at the end of the school year, some over the summer and some may even assume their new position mid-year, which could be a challenge, but one must always be ready and have a plan of action to take these initial steps whenever the opportunity arises.

In addition to meeting your staff, it is always helpful to gain their perspective and reality of the organization. This process is critical before moving forward with any plan because it will expose or highlight areas that should remain untouched and priority areas in need of immediate attention. As a new leader, it is not recommended to change everything at once, so focus on the most significant areas first. It could become detrimental to the culture of the organization to do a complete overhaul immediately, with little to no input. You must prioritize and know where to start and go from there. Remember, effective transformation is a marathon and not a sprint. Areas that are highly valued by the organization and are yielding positive results should be left in place. The fewer changes, the less likely you are to disrupt the main flow of the organization. However, the areas that are not producing good results for the organization should be addressed at once, with a logical explanation as to why the change is happening along with the benefits of those changes. Clearly communicating why the change is happening and the plan for implementation is the most valuable action a leader can take.

As stated earlier, the most effective way of determining what is highly valued to an organization and areas in need of immediate attention is to have the staff complete a survey or host a brief face-to-face conference before your official first day on the job (if applicable). If you are not able to survey or meet with the employees prior to the beginning of the school year, the first two weeks is also an opportune time to gather information. The survey or face-to-face interviews will give employees a set aside time to share their values and concerns with you as their new leader. This process will also make them feel like their voice/opinion matters and allows for an opportunity to build rapport with new employees. This practice will also provide insight on the personalities in the organization and the type of leader they feel they need. Great initial questions to ask whether written or oral are:

1) Describe the organization in four words and its goals.
2) What do you like most about working at_____?
3) What are some areas for improvement or growth?
4) What advice would you give to me as a new leader?

Each question will yield a novice leader very pertinent information. For example, Question #1: Describe the organization in four words and its goals, yields their perception on how they perceive the organization. It will also allow the staff to share what they believe their values and core beliefs are if any. If the organization is strong, their mission and vision should be clearly highlighted at this time, and there should be common threads shared from person to person.

Question #2: What do you like most about working at _____? This question will allow for the positive aspects of the organization to be pinpointed and highlight what is important to the faculty. This question is probably the most important because as answers are given, you must look for commonalities that should be left untouched if possible. Most times, what people like most about an organization is what creates the culture. Culture plays a big part in how an organization functions but is overlooked way too often. Culture can be summarized as the social habits, attitudes, beliefs and customs that differentiate one group of people from another. In other words, it is the soul of the organization. As a leader you must know the existing culture to understand how you will best serve and cultivate the group. In my experience, an unhealthy culture in a building is the hardest and most troublesome to change. But if the culture is healthy and thriving, it can be the number one thing you love most about working at the building.

Question #3: What are some areas of improvement? This question is probably the second most important to ask because once the employees have given you areas of concerns and you see the commonalities, when you go to resolve the issues, you can highlight them as a response to their concerns rather than something you are changing. This gesture will make the transition smoother and more acceptable for the employees.

Finally, Question #4: What advice would you give to me as a new leader? Everyone wants to feel like they have been heard and this question allows for employees to give advice because they have been asked. This allows for need-to-know information to be given from the viewpoint of the employees.

If you had 50 employees and during the beginning stages took the time to administer this survey, think about all the knowledge you would have to aid you in your decision-making journey as the new leader or administrator. Many people fail to take the time to initiate this process and spend years repairing or rebuilding relationships because they didn't take the time to gain proper insight from the start.

Conditioning Tip #4: Sharpen Your People Skills.

Effective leadership requires you to be an extrovert most of the time. If you find yourself to be withdrawn or timid, leadership may not be the profession for you because it requires strength and advocacy at several levels. You will spend most of your day talking to people from various backgrounds immersed in unique opinions. Therefore, you will have to be knowledgeable, relatable, approachable and most importantly able to take a stand in difficult situations.

DR. HUNTER'S CORNER

Although taking the time to initially gain input from staff can be time consuming, it will pay off later and allow for an easier transition into the role by providing you with a point of reference. Also, it allows personal insight into personalities, expectations and perspectives, which will aid you in building authentic relationships.

I executed this process when I took on the role as principal. It took me about two weeks to have one-on-one meetings with each staff member, but I gained so much from the experience. I scheduled the meetings and created a warm and safe environment for them to share their likes and concerns. A lot of the changes I implemented came from the survey and the reoccurring responses they provided. I truly believe that even though I experienced a little push back in the beginning from the "never-changing nay-sayers", the majority clearly understood why I was making the changes and minimized the separation that can sometimes happen when new leadership arrives. As a leader, you will face adversity, but be proactive in finding ways to minimize the casualties that may result from the peer pressure from those who will never get onboard.

Questions To Ask Yourself As You Reflect on Chapter 4:

Q1: Am I an introvert or an extrovert? How will this help or hurt my ability to build strong foundations with my team?

Q2: How important is someone else's perspective to me?

Q3: How do I show others that I value their opinion?

Q4: What will be my plan to become acclimated to the organization in the first few weeks?

Q5: What information would you include in your first introduction to the staff? *Drafting a preliminary presentation or introductory letter could assist you in preparing.*

CHAPTER 5

EFFECTIVE COMMUNICATION

After building the initial rapport and getting to know the staff's perceptions and perspectives, an effective ongoing communication plan must be developed. Research highlights most plans fail at the implementation phase of which effective communication is identified as the heartbeat. Communication is very important when building a strong foundation and is critical to every organization. Now that you have received valuable information from the staff about the strengths and weaknesses of the organization, reviewed the mission and vision of the school, studied supporting documents and performance data, and have probably identified the all-stars and naysayers, it is time to plan your year and clearly communicate the road ahead with all staff. An effective transformational leader should first communicate the findings from solicited staff's input. Secondly, list the areas you believe need to be addressed and areas that should remain intact, which should be supported by factual information. Third, review the mission and vision of the organization. Fourth, identify and communicate your non-negotiables, expectations and finally, the way ahead. Although you will never receive a 100% approval rating as a leader, when you take the time to properly communicate the What, When, Who, How and most importantly, Why, you are more likely to have the majority support your initiatives.

#1 Communicating Your Findings From Solicited Input

Everyone likes to feel his or her opinion is valued, and voice is heard. By taking the initial steps to ask the staff their opinion about the strengths and growth opportunities of the organization, you have won half the battle. Once you have obtained all the information and have tallied the recurring themes, it is now time to list your concerns and acknowledge the great things that are going on. Next, you must prioritize the items that need to be addressed immediately and those that will be addressed in the future, recognizing you will not be able to address everything all at once. A good way to help identify which concern makes which list is by using your vision and mission to help you decide. Another way to determine where to start is by assessing what will make the most significant improvements the fastest and will ultimately impact the culture and student achievement. Once you have your list, you will have to communicate your findings to the staff. A good way to share the information is during your first official meeting with the staff via PowerPoint or multimedia presentation. Graphs and charts are great visuals to communicate findings. Share with the staff how many people you interviewed, the overall answers given (those that were of a significant number, avoid the answers that were of very few opinions to help with relevancy and time), the common recurring themes that came up for each question (noting the number of responses, but no names), and "WHY" you gathered the information. An example would be: 42 of the 50 staff members stated they loved the Wednesday morning professional learning communities (PLC) meetings, and 30 of the 50 reported they would like to see more professional development for parents. Avoid statements like 2 of the 50 stated that... for the sake of time.

#2 Communicating Your Priorities

After communicating to the staff what their responses were, next you should share what you believe would be the opportunities for growth based on their responses and supporting data, documents and other pertinent information you may have obtained, and what you believe needs to remain intact and why. It is important to celebrate the positives and strengths of the organization during this stage because the staff needs to see that several things are remaining in place. It is also equally important to share why the areas being addressed are considered your priorities. One way of doing this is by reviewing the vision and mission of the organization, which should support your ideology.

#3 Communicating the Vision and Mission

Following your list of priorities, it is important to make the connections to how the list of improvements supports the vision and mission of the school. ASCD (formerly The Association for Supervision and Curriculum Development) highlights that your school must have a vision that all staff members recognize as a common direction of growth. It is something that inspires them to be better and announces to parents and students where you are heading and why they should take the trip with you. Without a vision, your school lacks direction. A mission is simply how you are going to carry the vision out. It is important to make sure that all staff are aware of the vision and mission and agree with it. If it was created properly, the staff should have developed it together and should therefore be a living document. If you find otherwise, ASCD notes a few questions to ponder are:

1) Is there a need for a new vision?

2) Will I be able to live with the new vision?

3) Will I be able to support the new vision?

4) What will the new vision expect of me?

5) How will my world change as a result?

6) Will I be able to continue doing what I've always done? Why or why not?

7) Do I believe in this new vision?

8) Do I believe in my school's ability to achieve this vision?

9) Do I believe I can help make the vision happen?

#4 Communicating the Non-Negotiables or Expectations

Now that the connections have been made, the staff should understand the improvements that will occur does not just come from "the new leader that is coming in and changing everything", which will be said by some of the staff members no matter what the process or journey to change will be, but comes from aligning the need for improvement with the platform that was created together. This way of thinking will only be effective if it matches your leadership style, which in this case would most closely align with the democratic way of leading versus the authoritative way. However, when beginning to communicate your non-negotiables or expectations, many may view the activity as authoritarian. However, it needs to be done.

Every transformational leader must have their non-negotiables because these are what anchor you as a leader. The non-negotiables are your core values and what makes you consistent during your tenure as administrator/leader. Non-negotiables cannot be changed by discussion and the staff must understand what they are. A few examples of non-negotiables are students first when making any decision, professionalism and respect when communicating with each other. By stating these non-negotiables or expectations up front, staff members will know how to proceed through the year without feeling offended when certain decisions are made. Leaders should also hold themselves to their non-negotiables to keep themselves from becoming political or personal. Some leaders may involve their staff members when coming up with the universal list of non-negotiables or expectations.

#5 Communicating the Way Ahead

Finally, it is most important to communicate the way ahead to staff as clearly and concisely as possible. Many people fear change because of the unknown. Therefore, a very detailed plan is necessary to move ahead in a productive manner. Sharing with staff what is changing, when it is expected to happen, who is responsible for carrying it out and how it will be done is necessary. You will have already explained the Why in the first steps by sharing the data, but feel free to revisit it at this stage if you feel the need to. You can never clarify too much. The leader must understand each of these areas fully before rolling out the plan. Some buildings have leadership teams you may want to consult with first to fail proof the plan because after all, they will be the ones to sell it to the rest of the staff to get the buy-in. You cannot implement significant changes in an organization alone or without support; you must first solicit the thoughts from those who will be working closest with you. This will make the transition smoother.

Conditioning Tip #5: Be a planner.

Start with the end in mind. Know where you want to take the organization and exactly how you are going to get them there. Remember where you lead, they will follow.

Communication Is Key To Building A Solid Foundation

Step 1
Introduce yourself to the staff to find out who they are.

Step 2
Find out their perceptions of the organization.

Step 3
Review your personal agreements before building any relationships.

Step 4
Review data and prioritize findings.

Step 5
Effectively communicate the way ahead.

DR. HUNTER'S CORNER

Communication is the key to effective leadership. No matter what capacity I lead in, it all begins with communication. I am very intrigued by people and the act of transformation, so I automatically ask a lot of questions. This trait has helped me a lot. In fact, I probably ask too many questions! I am reminded of a time when I first started a leadership position at a new job and I sat in an executive leadership meeting doing what I know to do, which was to ask the "hard" questions. I was told I needed to stop before I rubbed others the "wrong way", but the truth was, it was tough for the others in the meeting to answer those questions that made them uncomfortable. However, I still asked and eventually they had to address them, which positively impacted future decisions that were made. So don't be afraid to speak up, even if your voice shakes.

I believe in the power of getting to the root cause of any problem in order to fix it. A strategy that has come in handy when trying to figure out where to start when addressing an issue is to ask "Why?" five times, and eventually you will get a good place to begin. Communication is an art. Many people struggle with it. They assume a lot and are not clear about the task or the way ahead, which leaves followers operating in the blind. Assess your communication skills and don't be afraid to find ways to enhance them.

Questions To Ask Yourself As You Reflect on Chapter 5:

Q1: How will I introduce myself to the staff?

Q2: How will I determine the elements of the organization that will remain and what will change?

Q3: How will I build the necessary rapport with the leadership team without compromising my position?

Q4: What are my non-negotiables or expectations and why do I feel so strongly about them?

CHAPTER 6

BUILDING RELATIONSHIPS THAT ARE PROFESSIONAL, FAIR AND RESPECTFUL

After taking the time to lay a solid foundation by gaining proper insight from each of your employees, the opportunity to begin developing healthy relationships will follow. Nurturing healthy and appropriate relationships for some leaders could pose many challenges, however, it is one of the most important aspects of the job. When building relationships, you must remember these two notions: 1) always remain professional and 2) treat everyone with respect and fairness.

Integrity *- the quality of being honest and fair. Adherence to moral and ethical principals.*

The advice of always remaining professional when you are in a leadership role is critical to your reputation and overall effectiveness as a leader. When you take on a leadership role, you are distinguished from the rest of the staff, not in a superior or demeaning manner, but in an executive role. Although some may believe being professional or overly professional does not allow for heartfelt relationships, there is a difference between being guarded, uptight and unwelcoming versus being warm and sincere, but with boundaries. Being professional means having limits that should not be crossed, certain topics that should not be discussed, language that should not be used and after-hour company that should not be held. As a leader you are to present yourself as one who is unbiased, knowledgeable, transparent and always committed. You should be able to enforce policies without hesitation, correct misbehavior when appropriate and make unpopular decisions for the greater good without fear of hurting feelings or dissolving relationships. When the lines of professionalism are blurred, it makes it very difficult for others to see you as their leader and respect your decisions. For example, having drinks with staff the night before or sharing private information about others while later promoting confidentiality in faculty meetings. It is very difficult to correct a friend or colleague when they start to see you more as their pal than their supervisor. The most effective leaders know how to keep the degrees of separation present, which in return, may cause loneliness.

There are plenty of ways to present yourself as kind hearted without becoming overly personal with staff. For example: through conversations held in passing, you could ask general questions about their family, so you can acknowledge birthdays, anniversaries, children's graduations, etc. Write thank you notes to acknowledge their great work and dedication, host retreats, but always remember other employees are watching your actions and would prefer to see a neutral boss who does not show favoritism or fraternize with the employees. Remain professional yet charismatic. This will help to build trust and respect with the staff, which leads to the second point of always treating everyone fair and with respect.

In most cases, fair does not always mean equal. Unfortunately, we do not live in a one-size-fit-all world. Therefore, there will be occasions when adjustments must be made when dealing with numerous individuals. They all have their special needs and therefore will not be able to be treated "the same." For example, the teacher who just had surgery should not be expected to attend the after-school dance or carnival hosted by PTO as everyone else would be. Each person is unique and has different needs. Just like accommodations and modifications are made for neurodivergent students to be successful, you will have to do the same for staff. It is critical that administrators convey this important message to those they serve.

However, no matter what the situation may be and what accommodations and modifications may have to be made, you should always be fair to everyone. When you make decisions for the group, you should always ask yourself, "What's fair?" Todd Whitaker pinned the thought-provoking question, "What will the best people think about your decision?" as a reminder to stay focused on the main goal, because it is so easy to try and please the status quo or choose the path of least resistance. Treating others fairly, no matter the cost, will leave you with no regrets. There will be times when you feel you need to make a decision that will go best with your plan or agenda, but when you really analyze the situation, you will find the decision may not be the fairest, which will cause you to change your decision. Respecting and treating a pretentious employee fair will be the hardest thing to do, but when you lead and serve with integrity, you will be able to do so with ease. Remember that leadership is a servanthood, and you are there to bring the best out in others, so respect is inevitable. Respect is important, and in order to get genuine respect, you need to give respect. Respect is something that should be given to everyone even when you may not think they deserve it because transformational leaders are conditioned to lead by example, often returning evil with good.

Conditioning Tip #6: Lead with integrity.

The more forthcoming and upright you are as a leader, the easier it is for others to respect you. Be firm but fair, professional but warm and respectful to everyone!

DR. HUNTER'S CORNER

I would have to say that building relationships is probably one of my most valuable strengths. If you believe in astrology, my zodiac sign is Libra, which means I'm all about balance, good energy, comfort and peace, which naturally come easy to me. However, on the other hand, my weakness would be confrontation. Therefore, in many instances in my personal life and even as a leader, I would often avoid hard conversations or reprimands for as long as I possibly could. This character trait impacted me negatively until I acknowledged it and became stronger at addressing issues.

My hardest two jobs/duties were firing someone or assigning a low evaluation rating. However, because I took the time to establish respectful and fair relationships from the beginning, regardless of the employee's/member's personality, the majority accepted the reprimand with little to no hostility. In fact, I still keep in contact with and have great relationships with former employees. That's the impact and effect of establishing respectful and fair relationships from the beginning before adversity arises!

<u>Questions To Ask Yourself As You Reflect on Chapter 6:</u>

Q1: What are my views on professionalism, respect and fairness in the workplace?

Q2: Do I struggle with any of the traits? If so, which one (s) and why?

Q3: How would I maintain boundaries with a close friend or family member in the work environment?

Q4: What should I do when I realize a relationship needs to be repaired because of the lack of professionalism, respect or fairness shown as the leader?

Q5: How and when should I practice integrity?

CHAPTER 7

GROWING PAINS: GOOD AND BAD DAYS

In every leadership position, there will be good days and bad days. Hopefully, during your tenure, you will find there are more good days than bad. The good days are the days that keep you going and grounded. On good days, your smile doesn't fade away, there's an extra skip to your step, the sweet sounds of birds are singing in your head and there is a melody in your heart. Good days are exhilarating and are highly sought after because the job of a leader is so demanding and consumes so much of who you are. You will need to experience as many good days and highs as possible. As a principal/leader, one of the best feelings ever is to be shown you are loved by the students, parents and staff.

Good days consist of students showing their appreciation for you by writing uplifting notes, bringing in unexpected gifts and greeting you with the biggest smiles and warmest hugs. Naturally, the lower the grade level, the more enthusiasm and personal interactions you will have. The older students tend to be more reserved in showing their emotions, yet you will know they care mostly through their smiles when they see you and a short note or quick compliment ever so often.

Parents can also show great appreciation and will make your day. Parents will let you know how much their child admires you and looks up to you as a role model and will let you know how your decisions have made a positive impact and have helped shape the climate at home. Most parents believe the employees at the school will take care of their most prized possession, so they expect the best from the teachers and principal. Also, parents show their appreciation and can make your day by being an active volunteer with the parent teacher organization (PTO) and may assist the school in any way needed. There is nothing like a supportive parent. When there is a strong, authentic relationship/partnership between the home and school, it makes all the difference in a child's academic and behavioral performance. Therefore, nurturing positive relationships between home and school is vital to the student's and school's overall success.

In addition to students and parents contributing to good days, it is also a great day when you have happy, dedicated teachers who bring fun and excitement to the school day. This will make any day a good day. There is nothing like everyone working together to achieve total success for all! Teachers can make the administrator's day with simple cards or emails saying, "Thank you." Teachers also create fantastic days when students are growing academically, and the test or assessment results show growth.

Additionally, good days happen when there are fun activities planned, so administrators should welcome spirit days to help with the culture and climate of the building. Simple things like Hat Day, Jean Day, and Award Day, create fun times at school. There is nothing like a good day! As an administrator, you go home feeling energized and ready for the next day. The good days remind you of why you give 110% all the time. Overall, these are signs the administrator has positively impacted the overall climate in the building and all things are coming together and aligning with the vision and mission of the school.

On the other hand, just like there are good days, there are also bad days or shall I say strained days. Strenuous days can be described as the "want to run home and pull the covers over your head days", the "why did I become an administrator/leader" days, the "they don't pay me enough for this" days, the "I am going to look for another job at the end of the year" days, which all lead to the "can't sleep at night" days, which is a result of what happened between the short hours of 6 A.M. and 4 P.M. Surprisingly, bad days can also originate from teachers, students and parents for a variety of reasons. Unfortunately, the stress that comes from the strained days may lead to chest pains, heartburn or restless nights. In fact, the high turnover rate in education is significantly connected to the increase of stress that comes from the "bad" days.

When you think about being a leader, your number one job is to be a problem solver. 90% of what you do during the day will be attached to solving problems. For example, when you first enter the building, sometimes teachers are waiting for you in the office to solve a problem, or a problem awaits you when you first open an email or listen to a phone message. There is always a problem lurking nearby, which will require your immediate attention and could cause you to become weary.

Teachers may contribute to draining days when they feel like they have received an unfavorable evaluation rating or had to be reprimanded for excessive tardiness, outlandish dress code, frequent absenteeism, lack of planning, etc. They can sometimes take their frustrations out on you by spreading negativity throughout the staff, refusing to abide by future directives and may even report you to the superintendent or central office leadership just to be revengeful. However, remember no matter how annoying their response may be, their attitudes reflect their issues from their perspective, so clear and thorough communication is warranted to help minimize the backlash. Explaining why and providing documentation after each behavior may be time consuming but will protect you later. Regardless of the documentation, retaliation causes most leaders to still worry and stress because they want to be liked. Leaders can feel hated when it appears that no one wants to talk to them or when the hallway gets quiet when they walk by. Nevertheless, continue to lead with integrity through the unwarranted tension. Remember, this too shall pass!

Policies- a definite course or method of action selected from among alternatives and in light of given conditions to guide and determine present and future.

In addition to teachers, students can often create challenging days by filling your schedule with disciplinary issues ranging from minor to major. However, no matter what, once the office referral comes, you must solve the problem and administer a consequence if deemed appropriate. The consequences may range from conferencing with a student to expulsion. This can be a very stressful time for the administrator because you want to make the right decision. Please be prepared and know you will not make everyone happy once the decision is made, so the best thing to do is to follow policies so you will not come across as biased or showing favoritism to the student or teacher. You must learn to make a decision and stand by it, while always being professional, respectful and fair. Remember, no matter how hard you try to do the right thing, you will not please everyone and that could make for an uneasy day.

Additionally, some parents may also cause an increase in stress. Nowadays most parents turn to social media to air their concerns, which can damage your reputation. However, in spite of the disrespect shown toward you, always strive to handle all parents with respect and fairness no matter their zip code. Sometimes, leaders tend to treat parents differently according to their job titles or relationships with other stakeholders such as central office staff, school board members, politicians, community leaders, etc. It is critical to examine biases and address them right away to prevent this from happening. Leaders are reminded that no matter how bad a situation may be, never discuss it publicly or in the front office with other staff members (teachers or secretaries) because it may be heard by bystanders.

One way to handle a hostile parent's response to an unfavorable decision is by establishing relationships ahead of time. Reaching out to parents by phone or in the carpool line just to say hi and check-in when there is no problem will help a lot in easing not so pleasant conversations. Research highlights most parents are only contacted when there is a discipline problem. Please refrain from doing this. Other ways that leaders can establish meaningful partnerships is by attending extracurricular activities or shopping in the local grocery stores. Once parents feel like you genuinely care about their child, they may respond less aggressively when a problem arises. On the other hand, be advised even after doing some of the aforementioned suggestions, there will still be parents who will respond in an unruly manner, but do not let it diminish your character.

Additional outliers that may cause stress is school performance scores. Leaders, know when you have worked very hard and the scores don't quite reflect the level of hard work that was done, it can affect your motivation and mental state. However, remember significant change doesn't happen overnight. In most cases, research says significant growth takes at least three to five years to manifest. If adequate work has been done, you should see some growth even if it is happening in small increments. No matter how small the win is, acknowledge it. This will serve as motivation for you and the staff to keep heading in that direction. Keep the data before the staff, so they can see progress and continue to trust in your leadership plan. However, do not neglect flexibility. When the results do not equate to the amount of work that was rendered, evaluate the actions, and change things up. When you are not getting the return on your investment, do not be afraid to change things that are not working or yielding the desired outcomes. Leadership requires you to be flexible and innovative. If you stay the course, respond strategically to the data, you will eventually see the change.

Leaders tend to be their biggest critic and making mistakes as a leader sometimes can cause undue stress. For example, forgetting about a deadline, or not having enough time to get everything done in the manner you would like to do it may cause you to stress. Save space for self-forgiveness. Remember you are only one person and can only do so much on your own. Pace yourself and do your best. Be okay with leaving work for the next day.

Self-care is critical in leadership. Keeping all matters in perspective is the only thing that will preserve your mental fortitude and longevity in the field of administration. To function at high levels, one must embrace the good days and remember to keep the bad ones in their proper place. Find ways to de-stress before arriving home to keep the burdens of the day from rolling over into your personal life. Remember, find another leader to serve as a confidant and sounding board. This will serve as a healthy way to leave troubles at work.

Conditioning Tip #7: Balance improves productivity.

Stress can manifest in multiple ways and sometimes affect your health. Balance is so important in leadership. Find ways to de-stress regularly.

DR. HUNTER'S CORNER

Although I have been told there is good stress and bad stress, I have never liked stress, even though I have always done well in stressful environments. Although I managed well, it took me a while to realize the impact that leadership was having on my physical health. I have endured many sleepless nights, headaches, angry parents and revengeful employees.

How do I maintain? I keep great company outside of work; pray morning, noon and night; focus on the positive while at work; play great music in my office; and have the best weekend fun. Whenever I receive cards and encouraging notes, I keep them visible to minimize the impact the bad days have on me. As time progresses, I have learned to keep everything in perspective and limit the amount of space "work" takes up in my overall life. Balance is key!

I have learned that no project or work problem is more important than your family. Therefore, remember to be present and show up for those who need you the most. Take breaks, breathe, laugh, miss a day or two when you are sick or need a mental health day; work will be there when you return. If you don't take care of yourself and your mental health, you will be no good for anyone else.

Questions To Ask Yourself As You Reflect on Chapter 7:

Q1: What are some things that make you happy? How can you incorporate those things into your day regularly?

Q2: What are some things that make you upset or uneasy? How can you control those things from affecting you at high levels?

Q3: How can you build positive relationships with your staff, students and parents?

CHAPTER 8

A REFLECTIVE LEADER: EVALUATION BIRTHS EVOLUTION

Being a transformational leader requires innovation, time, grit and perseverance. It takes a special person to go into an organization, conquer the politics, build effective relationships and partnerships, and get desired results. The true measure of success should be dependent upon the lives that were impacted in a positive manner under your tutelage. Sometimes leaders assess the effectiveness of their leadership capabilities solely on the school's test scores or what some may call numbers. However, leadership is so much more than that! Leadership is going beyond the managerial aspects of being a principal. It is sharing words of wisdom to all you meet. Leadership is making those around you feel valued and seen. It is creating a path for success and showing the followers how to get there. Leadership is allowing the "Why" to lead every decision you make, while keeping the students at the heart of those decisions. Authentic leadership is being courageous enough to accept the hard truth about yourself and the organization and being determined enough to transform it for the greater good.

Evaluation should bring evolution! Take the time to reflect on your experiences daily and annually. Transformational leaders continue to look for ways to simply make things better. Although the road may be a perplexing journey, remain up for the challenge. Reflecting daily on wins and losses is critical to evolving into the leader you aspire to be. Take the time to reflect on what went well and what could have been done better. It does not happen overnight, but with dedication and hard work, nothing is impossible. Leadership is a craft and to master it, one must put in the time to be conditioned.

Conditioning requires you to take the time on the front end to prepare yourself mentally, physically and spiritually. Becoming knowledgeable of your responsibilities is only the beginning; you must decide which type of leader you will be, equip yourself to be open minded to see other's perspectives, while always addressing any biases that may exist while refining your communication skills. Being professional and fair will provide longevity in your leadership role and strengthen your ability to handle stress at optimum levels. If you do these things, your foundation will be strong, and your preparation will lead you to the path of success. Finally, in all that you do, remember leadership has POWER and goes beyond the paycheck!

REFERENCES

ASCD (formerly The Association for Supervision and Curriculum Development)

Klein, A. (2021) *1,500 decisions a day (at least!): How teachers cope with a dizzying array of questions, Education Week*. Available at: https://www.edweek.org/teaching-learning/1-500-decisions-a-day-at-least-how-teachers-cope-with-a-dizzying-array-of-questions/2021/12 (Accessed: 29 November 2023).

Maxwell, John C. 2011. *The 5 Levels of Leadership : Proven Steps to Maximize Your Potential*. New York: Center Street.

Whitaker, Todd. 2013. *What Great Teachers Do Differently*. Routledge.

CPSIA information can be obtained
at www.ICGtesting.com
Printed in the USA
LVHW011546301122
733863LV00018B/990/J